A LIFE OF TOTAL PRAYER

Selected Writings of
CATHERINE OF SIENA

Upper Room Spiritual Classics® — Series 3

Selected, edited, and introduced by
Keith Beasley-Topliffe

UPPER
ROOM BOOKS™
NASHVILLE

A Life of Total Prayer:
Selected Writings of Catherine of Siena

The Upper Room® Website: http://www.upperroom.org

Cover design: Gore Studio, Inc.
Interior design and layout: Nancy J. Cole

First printing: 2000

Library of Congress Cataloging-in-Publication Data

Catherine, of Siena, Saint, 1347–1380.
    [Selection. English. 2000]
    A life of total prayer : selected writings of Catherine of Siena /
selected, edited, and introduced by Keith Beasley-Topliffe.
      p. cm. — (Upper Room spiritual classics. Series 3)
    ISBN 0-8358-0903-X
    1. Spiritual life—Catholic authors. I. Beasley-Topliffe, Keith.
II. Title. III. Series.
BX2349.C37213 2000
248.4'82—dc21   99-40407
                                        CIP

Printed in the United States of America

TABLE OF CONTENTS

INTRODUCTION

Saint Paul urged Christians, "Present your bodies as a living sacrifice, holy and acceptable to God" (Rom. 12:1). Thirteen centuries later, Catherine of Siena tried to live according to Paul's word. She drove herself tirelessly for the reconciliation of enemies and the reform of the church, offering her physical sufferings as atonement for the sins of others. With Paul, she could truly say, "In my flesh I am completing what is lacking in Christ's afflictions for the sake of his body, that is, the church" (Col. 1:24).

This self-sacrifice was driven by a burning desire to submit her will completely to God's will for her. This, in turn, was fueled by a prayer life so intense that she often lost all consciousness of the world around her. Even in the midst of dictating letters, she sometimes burst into prayer and praise.

Fortunately Catherine was very good at putting her experiences into words. She wrote hundreds of letters to friends and religious and government leaders. Whatever the occasion, her writing always moved on to deeper matters, urging her correspondents to turn away from sin and draw nearer to God. Her teaching earned her the title of Doctor of the Church, one of the first two women (the other was Teresa of Avila) to be so honored.

CATHERINE'S WORLD

The fourteenth century was a tumultuous time in Italy and throughout Europe. Several years of poor crops were followed in 1348 by the Black Death, an epidemic of bubonic plague that killed one-third of the people of Europe. Bands of mercenary soldiers that helped cities to pursue feuds with neighbors turned to banditry when no one would hire them. Many cities in central Italy, though officially subject to either the pope or the Holy Roman emperor, had a great amount of self-government and very turbulent politics. One of these city-republics was Siena, about 180 miles north of Rome and 43 south of Florence.

The church reached a high point in the twelfth century. The pope was powerful enough to demand and receive penance from kings, but his power declined drastically by the early fourteenth century. In 1303 the king of France forced the election of a French pope, the first of several. In 1309 Pope Clement V moved his headquarters from Rome to Avignon in southern France. That was the beginning of the so-called Babylonian Captivity of the church. For nearly seventy years the papacy was controlled by the French monarchy, and the pope's territory in central Italy was ruled by proxies, often French bishops. Several cities, led by Florence and Milan, rebelled against papal authority.

At the end of the twelfth century, Dominic and Francis founded orders of friars who helped to revitalize the church with enthusiasm and scholarship.

Both orders established universities and produced outstanding theologians in the Franciscan Bonaventure and the Dominican Thomas Aquinas. By the fourteenth century, the orders became institutionalized and scholarship stagnated. Still, the Dominicans in Siena maintained a standard of theological training and preaching through which Catherine absorbed a first-rate education.

CATHERINE'S LIFE

Catherine Benincasa was born March 25, 1347, the twenty-third of twenty-four children born to Giacomo di Benincasa, a cloth dyer, and his wife, Lapa. A twin sister died in infancy. The next year the Black Death came to Siena, killing half the people. When she was six, Catherine had a vision of Christ that led her to dedicate her life to God. As a child she practiced a variety of devotions, tempered somewhat by the desire to be a typical girl.

In 1362, when she was fifteen, Catherine cut her hair to discourage her parents' plans for her marriage, and she began to live as a servant in her home. Two years later she became one of the Mantellate, a Dominican lay order of women (primarily older widows) who took special vows and who were named for the cloaks (*mantella*) they wore in public. As an unmarried teenager, Catherine needed special permission to join the order. For the next three years she remained primarily in her room in prayer. She left each morning to attend Mass, where she sometimes each morning to attend Mass, where she sometimes went into ecstasy and had to be carried out at the end of the service. Often she did housework while her family slept. By this time she ate only bread, water, and raw vegetables. She wanted to be able to read, but struggled to learn her letters. She prayed for help and found she could read from then on.

At the beginning of Lent in 1368, Catherine had a vision in which Christ took her as his bride. At the same time, Christ sent her out of solitude to a life of service. At first she worked in the hospitals of Siena. By that point, she had gathered a circle of friends — male and female, clergy and lay — who looked to her for guidance, calling her "Mama." As her prayer life intensified, she became less able to tolerate earthly food. She stopped eating bread in 1370 and could not keep down any solid food after 1372.

After the return of the Black Death to Siena in 1374, Catherine felt called to go beyond service to individuals to serve the church as a whole and the people of Italy in particular. She had three overriding concerns. She supported a call for a new crusade in the hope that those who wanted to fight would do so in the Holy Land and for a holy cause. She urged the pope to return to Rome. And she called for the reform of the church. The crusade never happened. But in 1376, Catherine traveled to Avignon to meet with Pope Gregory XI. Her attempt to mediate the dispute with Florence and its allies failed, but the pope left Avignon for Rome in September. Catherine returned to Siena. She learned to write and began to work on her book, the *Dialogue*, which she completed by October 1378.

In the meantime, Gregory XI died. His successor, Urban VI, pushed so strongly for sweeping reforms that many of the cardinals turned against him and elected their own pope, Clement VII. Urban called Catherine to Rome to lend her support to his cause. She and her large group of disciples lived as a community under her direction. Catherine's health was in a precarious condition. She had to spend much of the time in bed, though she still rallied her strength to walk to Mass at Saint Peter's each day. She was completely unable to eat or drink water by January 1380. Yet she lived through Lent, continuing to dictate letters supporting reform and unity in the church. She died in Rome on April 29, 1380, at the age of thirty-three. She was buried in a tomb in the church of Santa Maria sopra Minerva, though her head was later removed and taken to Siena. She was declared a saint in 1461.

FURTHER READING

See the "Note on the Texts" for information on Catherine's writings.

The first biography of Catherine was written by her confessor, Raymondo da Capua, soon after her death. A couple of recent translations are available. The best modern biographies are by Johannes Jörgenson (translated by Ingeborg Lund) and Sigrid Undset (translated by Kate Austin-Lund), though both may be hard to find. Suzanne Noffke's *Catherine of Siena: Vision Through a Distant Eye* (Liturgical Press, 1996) is an excellent introduction to Catherine's life and thought and includes a travelogue of places in Italy connected with Catherine.

Barbara Tuchman's *A Distant Mirror: The Calamitous Fourteenth Century* offers a thorough look at Catherine's time, including a discussion of the Avignon "captivity" and Catherine's part in ending it.

Catherine's theology was greatly influenced by the writings of Thomas Aquinas, available in a variety of editions. Spiritual writers who were contemporaries include Julian of Norwich and the author of *The Cloud of Unknowing*.

NOTE ON THE TEXTS

The selections from the *Dialogue* are taken from the 1907 translation by Algar Thorold, available on the Internet at the Christian Classics Ethereal Library. It omits more than one-third of the book. These selections have been edited for modern grammar, vocabulary, and inclusive language. Paulist Press has published a complete and modern translation by Suzanne Noffke.

Noffke is the translator for the first five selections from Catherine's letters, taken from the first of a projected four-volume annotated set from the Center for Medieval and Early Renaissance Studies at SUNY Binghamton. When completed, it will be the first complete English translation of Catherine's letters, but only one volume has been published. The final selection from a letter was translated by Kenelm Foster and Mary John Ronayne in *I, Catherine*, published by Collins. These letters have been edited for length only. Catherine's letters were numbered in an edition of 1860 by Niccola Tomaseo. These numbers are given (as T29, etc.) for cross-reference with other collections.

Catherine's use of Scripture is very free. The translators have followed her own Italian. No attempt has been made to conform with a standard translation.

LEARNING TO LOVE

From a letter (T29) to Regina della Scala of Milan (late 1373)

In 1373, Bernabo Visconti, the tyrant of Milan, sent ambassadors to urge Siena to join an antipapal league. Catherine wrote to Visconti urging him to give up this plan and submit to the authority (secular as well as spiritual) of the pope, whom she refers to as "Christ on earth." She also wrote a long letter to his wife, Regina della Scala, in hopes that she might persuade her husband to a more holy life. This selection and the next come from that letter.

In the name of Jesus Christ crucified and of gentle Mary.

Revered mother in Christ Jesus,

I Caterina, servant and slave of the servants of Jesus Christ, am writing to you in his precious blood. I long to see you so clothed in the garment of blazing charity that you may be the means and instrument of reconciling your husband with Christ gentle Jesus and with his vicar, Christ on earth. I am certain that if charity is strong in you, your husband cannot fail to feel its warmth. This is what First Truth wants: that the two of you share one spirit, one affection, one holy desire. And without the love of charity this is beyond your reach.

But you will say to me, "Since I have no such love, and without it I am powerless, how can I get it?" I will tell you. Love is had only by loving. If you want love, you must begin by loving — I mean you must want to love. Once you want it, you must open the eye of your understanding to see where and how love is to be found. And you will find it within your very self. How? When you recognize your nothingness. And once you see that of yourself you do not even exist, you will recognize and appreciate that God is the source of your existence and of every favor above and beyond that existence — God's graces and gifts both temporal and spiritual. For without existence, we would not be able to receive any grace at all. So everything we have, everything we discover within ourselves, is indeed the gift of God's boundless goodness and charity.

This discovery and sight of our Creator's tremendous goodness to us makes us rise to such a growth of love and desire that we count as nothing — even despise — ourselves and the world and all the world's pleasures. This doesn't surprise me, because this is love's way, that when we see ourselves loved we love in return. And because we love, we would rather die than offend the one we love. We are fed in love's fire because we realize how loved we are when we see that we ourselves were the soil and the rock that held the standard of the most holy cross. For you know very well that neither earth nor rock could have held the cross, nor could cross or nails have held God's only-begotten Son, had not love held him fast. So God's love for our souls was the rock and the nails that held him fast.

This then is how we find love. And how are we to love once we have discovered where love is? Oh dearest revered mother, he himself is the rule and the way. There is no other. If we would walk in the light and receive the life of grace, the way he teaches us to follow—his way—is to go the path of suffering, the path of disgrace, derision, torment, ridicule, and persecution. It is by such suffering that we become conformed with Christ crucified. He is the spotless Lamb who scorned the world's wealth and power. He was the God-Man; yet, as our rule and our way, he teaches us by becoming himself a fulfiller, not an abolisher, of the Law. He is humble and meek, for never a cry or complaint is heard from him. In the greatness of his love he has opened himself up. Our salvation becomes his food and delight as he neither considers nor seeks himself but only the Father's honor and other people's welfare. He does not evade suffering but walks right up to it.

It is an awesome thing to see the good gentle Jesus, the one who rules and feeds the whole universe, in such great want and need that no one else has ever been as poor as he. He is so poor that Mary hasn't a blanket to wrap him in. In the end he dies naked on the cross so that he might reclothe us and cover our nakedness. Our sin had left us naked; we had lost the garment of grace. So Jesus gave up his own life and with it clothed us. I tell you, then, the soul who has discovered love in the love of Christ crucified will be ashamed to pursue it in any other way than that of Christ crucified. She will not want pleasure, status, or pomp, but will prefer to be like a pilgrim or traveler in this life, with her attention focused wholly on reaching her journey's goal. And if she is a good pilgrim, neither any prosperity she may encounter along the way nor any difficulty will slow her down. No, she will go forward bravely in love and in eagerness for the goal she hopes to reach.

LOVING GOD, NOT THINGS

From a letter (T29) to Regina della Scala of Milan (continued)

This selection is a later portion of the letter. Here she addresses the subject of avarice, for which Regina della Scala was notorious.

Use the things of this world as nature needs them, but not with excessive attachment. For it would be very displeasing to God if you were to set your heart on something of less value than yourself. That would be nothing but a surrender of your dignity. For people become like what they love. If I love sin, which is nothingness, I too become a nothing. I cannot fall any lower than that.

Sin arises simply from loving what God hates and hating what God loves. So if you love the passing things of this world and love yourself with a sensual love, you sin. For this is what God hates; in fact, it so displeases him that he willed to work out vengeance and punishment for it upon his own body. He made himself an anvil, and on this anvil hammered out our sins.

How great, then, is our wretched blindness! We see that we were created in God's image and likeness and later formed anew in grace. (He formed his image in us anew by the outpouring of his blood after we had lost it by deadly sin.) Yet we are so blind as to abandon God's affection and love which in his goodness made us so great, and give ourselves over to loving things apart from God! I mean we take our affection and love away from God to love ourselves and created things without God! It is not that prestige and worldly pleasure and other people are evil in themselves; what is evil is our attachment to them when by such attachment we disregard the sweet commandment of God. When, on the other hand, our affection and love are turned away from ourselves and centered entirely in Christ crucified, we achieve the greatest dignity possible to us, because we become one with our Creator. What greater good could there be than union with him who is all good? We cannot attribute the dignity of that union to ourselves, however; love is responsible for it. A servant maid would become a great lady should the emperor make her his wife. By her union with him she would become an empress—not by her own merit (for she was only a servant), but because of his dignity as emperor. Just think, dearest mother in Christ gentle Jesus! The soul who has fallen in love with God, she who is a servant and slave ransomed by the blood of God's Son, attains such great dignity that she cannot be called a servant now, but an empress, spouse of the eternal emperor! How well this agrees with the words of First Truth: "To serve God is not to be a slave but to reign"! For God rescues her from the servitude of sin and makes her free. This perfect union is indeed powerful, for it completes the basic dignity of being, of having been created by God, by uniting the soul in love and virtue with her Creator. Such a soul has been stripped of her old self and has been clothed in a new self, in Christ gentle Jesus. Then she is open to receive and hold that grace by which she experiences God in this life, and in the end enjoys the sight of him eternally. There she is at peace, in perfect rest and quiet, for her desires are fulfilled.

The reason we cannot have this sort of peace in this life is that our desire is not completely satisfied until we reach this union with the divine Being. As long as we are pilgrim travelers in this life we have only desire and hunger: desire to follow the right path, and hunger to reach our final destination. This desire makes us run along the way, the road cemented by Christ crucified. For if we had no love for God as our destination, we would have no concern for wanting to know the way.

I want you, then, to have an ever greater true holy desire to follow this way, the road that will bring you to your destination. Know that this road is not dark and gloomy or overgrown with thorns. It is lighted by the true light, Jesus Christ, who cemented this road with his own blood. There are no thorns here because this road is fragrant with a profusion of flowers and delicious fruits — so much so that once a person sets out along that pleasant roadway, she experiences such delight there that she would rather die than deliberately leave it. And though thorns may appear on this road (the seeming thorns of the devil's frequent annoyances and deceits), and though the world may flaunt itself before us with its inflated pride, yet I say the soul who finds her delight on this road is not bothered by these things. Rather she does as one who goes to a rosebush and picks the rose, letting the thorns be. So she leaves behind the troubles and anxieties of the world and picks the fragrant rose of true holy patience, setting before her mind's eye the life-giving blood of the Lamb, set before us on this road.

So run, mother! And let all true faithful Christians run to this blood, attracted by its fragrance. Then we will get really drunk on this blood, afire and consumed in gentle divine charity, made one with him. We will be like a heavy drinker, who thinks not of himself but only of the wine he has drunk and of what he still has left to drink. Get drunk on the blood of Christ crucified! Don't let yourself die of thirst when you have it right there before you! And don't take just a little, but enough to make you so drunk that you will lose yourself. Love yourself not selfishly but for God's sake. Love other people not for their sake but only for the praise and glory of God's name. Love God not for your own sake, for your own profit, but love him for his sake, because he is the highest Good and is worthy of being loved. Then your love will be perfect and not mercenary. You will be unable to think of anything except Christ crucified and the wine you have drunk — that is, the perfect charity which you see God has shown and given you before the creation of the world, since he was in love with you before you even came to be. If he had not so fallen in love with you he would never have created you. But because of the love he had for you as he saw you within himself, he was moved to grant you being. How your thoughts will be stretched when you drink this charity! I mean you will be thinking about what there is still to drink, eagerly desiring to taste and possess the supreme eternal beauty of God.

ARMOR AGAINST EVIL

From a letter (T148) to Pietro del Monte Santa Maria of Siena (summer 1375)

Pietro del Monte Santa Maria was one of the leading citizens of Siena. In this letter Catherine plays upon the traditionally "masculine" virtues (courage, boldness, etc.) to urge Pietro to be a knight for Christ on the spiritual battlefield.

In the name of Jesus Christ crucified and of gentle Mary.

Very revered and dearest father and son in Christ gentle Jesus,

I Caterina, servant and slave of the servants of Jesus Christ, am writing to you in the precious blood of God's Son. I long to see you a courageous and fearless knight. A man who knows he is well armed ought not be afraid. Oh dearest son, we see that God has equipped us with armor so strong that it cannot be pierced by the devil or anyone else. That armor is our free will, and this is the freedom God refers to when he says, "I created you without your help, but I will not save you without your help."

Now God wants us to make use of the armor he has given us; he wants us to deflect with it the blows our enemies inflict on us. We have three specific enemies: the world, the flesh, and the devil. But let's not be afraid, because divine providence has outfitted us so well that we have no reason for fear. Our armor is good, and our helper the best. For our helper is God, and he is such that no one can withstand him. As long as we continue to look to this strong loving helper, we cannot be weakened by the thought of our own frailty. It seems this is what that dear lover Paul saw when he said, "I can do all things in Christ crucified, who is in me and strengthens me." For when Paul felt the annoyance and pricking of the flesh, he found strength not in himself, because he knew he was weak, but in Christ Jesus. It was because of Christ Jesus and that fine strong armor God had given him, his strong freedom, that he could say, "I can do all things." For neither the devil nor anyone else can force me to commit a single deadly sin against my will. We can never be overcome unless we give up this armor and turn it over to the devil by our willing consent. The temptations and wiles of the devils, the flesh, and the world may come shooting poisoned arrows—the flesh with ugly thoughts and sensations, the devil with his assorted temptations and deceit and trickery, the world with its pretentiousness and pride. But unless lady freedom consents to these disordered suggestions, she never sins, because sin is in the will alone. And God has given us this as a favor, not as our due.

I don't want you to be afraid, no matter what you may experience, my dear son in Christ Jesus, because God has so favored us that he himself is our helper, and he has given us good armor. Even more: he was in the end dead yet victorious on the battle-field—dead because he died on the wood of the most holy cross, victorious because by his death he gave us life. He returned to the city of his eternal Father with his spouse as his spoils, I mean with our souls, whom God espoused when he took our human nature. Well may we focus our mind's eye, wide open, on such a fire of love! Our enemies have been conquered! We have been snatched from the hands of the devils who possessed us and held our souls as their own. Christ conquered the world and pride by stooping down to our humanity. And the flesh has been conquered by his enduring suffering and disgrace, insults and wrongs, torments and ridicule, abuse and death for us. So we may well be encouraged, since our enemies have been conquered!

Let us follow in his footsteps, driving out vice by virtue: pride by humility, impatience by patience, injustice by justice, impurity by perfect chastity and continence, vainglory by God's honor and glory—so that whatever we do and accomplish may be for the glory, praise, honor, and spread of our Jesus' name. Let a sweet holy war be waged against these vices!

clotheD In the fIRe of love

From a letter (T108) to Monna Giovanna di Capo
and Francesca in Siena (late 1375)

*Giovanna and Francesca were two of the Mantellate of
Siena. Catherine urges them to increase their devotion until
they are consumed in the fire of divine love.*

In the name of Jesus Christ crucified and of gentle
Mary.

My dearest and very loved daughters,

I Caterina, servant and slave of the servants of
Jesus Christ, am writing to you in his precious blood.
I long to see you so thoroughly ablaze and consumed
in the fire of divine charity that all selfish love, all
coldheartedness, all spiritual darkness must be driven
out. What is divine charity like? It is always working,
never gets tired. It is like the money lender, always
making a profit on time: if he sleeps, he is making a
profit; if he eats, he is making a profit. Whatever he
does, he is making a profit; he never wastes time. It
isn't the money lender who does the work; it is his
treasure, time. This is how the loving spouse of Christ
acts when she is ablaze with divine charity: she is
always making a profit, and is never idle. She sleeps
and charity does the work. Eating, sleeping, keeping
vigil—everything she does is fruitful for her. Oh

charity, full of joy! You are a mother nourishing the virtues as children at your breast. You are rich beyond all wealth, so rich that the soul clothed in you cannot be poor. You give her your beauty because you make her one with you. For, as Saint John says, God is charity, and those who live in charity live in God, and God lives in them.

Oh dearest daughters, my soul's gladness and joy, consider your excellence and dignity, which you received from God through this mother charity! For God's love for his creatures was so strong that it moved him to draw us out of himself and give us, us, his own image and likeness—just so we might experience and enjoy him, and share in his eternal beauty. He did not make us animals without memory or understanding, but gave us memory to hold fast his benefits, and understanding to comprehend his supreme eternal will—his will that seeks nothing else but that we be made holy. And he gave us our will to love that will of his.

The will of the Word wants us to follow him on the way of the most holy cross by enduring every pain, abuse, insult, and reproach for Christ crucified, who is in us to strengthen us. And as soon as our understanding's eye perceives this, our will gets up at once. Warmed by the fire of this mother charity, it runs to love what God loves and hate what God hates, wanting to seek and desire and clothe itself in nothing but God's eternal will. Once we have seen and understood that God wants only our good, we see that it is God's will and pleasure to be followed on the way of the cross. We rejoice and are content with whatever God permits: sickness or poverty, insult or abuse, intolerable or unreasonable commands. We rejoice and are glad in everything, and we see that God permits these things for our profit and perfection. I'm not surprised that we are, then, free from suffering, since we have shed the cause of suffering— I mean self-will grounded in self-centeredness—and have put on God's will grounded in charity.

If you should say to me, "Mother, how shall we clothe ourselves?" I answer, "With hatred and with love." For love makes us put on love. It is just like a person who changes clothes, who is quick to take off old clothes in dislike for them, and with love put on new ones. My daughters, is it really the clothes the person is putting on? No, it is love, because clothes wouldn't get changed of their own accord. The person had to choose them out of love. And this hatred— where can we get it? Only from knowledge of ourselves, from recognizing that we are nothing. This is what banishes all pride and infuses true humility. This knowledge lets us discover the light and the generosity of God's goodness and boundless charity. This is not hidden from us. It was, of course, hidden to our coarseness until the Word, God's only-begotten Son, became incarnate. But once he had chosen to be our brother, clothing himself in the coarseness of our humanity, it was revealed to us. Then he was lifted up so that the fire of love might be revealed to all people and their hearts be attracted by love's power. So it is certainly true that love transforms and makes the beloved one with the lover.

So be eager, my daughters, to reach out with arms of love to seize and store away in your memory what your understanding has grasped. This is how God's desire and mine for you will be fulfilled. I mean I shall see you ablaze and consumed, clothed in the fire of divine charity. See to it, please do, that you nourish yourselves on blood, so that our time may come soon.

Don't be surprised that we haven't come. We will come soon, if it so pleases divine Goodness. I have delayed my coming a bit for the sake of a certain service to the Church and because the holy father wanted it. I beg you, I command you all, daughters and sons, to pray, to offer holy prayers and fervent desires to God for holy Church for she is much persecuted. I'll say no more. Keep living in God's holy and tender love.

Gentle Jesus! Jesus love!

ThE CELL OF
SELF-KNOWLEDGE

From a letter (T241) to Monna Giovanna di Corrado
From Maconi in Siena (summer 1376)

---

*Giovanna was the mother of one of Catherine's disciples,
Stefano Maconi. Stefano went with Catherine to Avignon.
Apparently Giovanna wrote to protest this separation from
her son. Catherine responded by urging her to go beyond her
motherly love to true love for God, a love she could find only
in the "cell of self-knowledge."*

In the name of Jesus Christ crucified and of gentle
Mary.

Dearest mother in Christ gentle Jesus,

I Caterina, servant and slave of the servants of
Jesus Christ, am writing to you in his precious blood.
I long to see you making your home in the cell of self-
knowledge, so that you may attain perfect love, for I
know that we cannot please our Creator unless we
love him, because he is love and wants nothing but
love. If we do know ourselves we find this love.
Why? Because we see our own nothingness, that our
very existence is ours by grace and not because we
have a right to it, and every grace beyond our existence as well—it is all given to us with boundless love.
Then we discover so much of God's goodness poured
out on us that words cannot describe it. And once we
see ourselves so loved by God, we cannot help loving
him. And within ourselves we love God and our

rationality, and hate the sensuality that would take inordinate pleasure in the world.

Some people delight in wealth or status, or would rather please creatures than the Creator. These build their foundation in worldly appearance, pleasure, and enjoyment. Then there are some who love their children or spouse or mother or father excessively, with too sensual a love. Such a love gets between their soul and God and keeps them from a clear knowledge of the truth of real heavenly love. This is why gentle First Truth said, "Unless you leave father and mother, sisters and brothers, and your very self, you are not worthy of me." God's true servants have always been very conscious of this, and quickly strip their heart, soul, and affection of the world and its pleasures and ostentation, and of loving anyone apart from God. Not that they don't love other people, but they love them only for God's sake, as creatures boundlessly loved by their Creator. But just as they hate in themselves the sensuality that rebels against God, so they hate this in their neighbors, for they see that it offends supreme eternal Good.

Here is what I want you to do, dearest mother in Christ gentle Jesus: to love God's goodness within yourself, and his immeasurable charity, which you will find in the cell of self-knowledge. In this cell you will find God. For just as God holds within himself everything that shares in being, so you will find within yourself memory, which holds and is well-suited to hold the treasure of God's blessing. There too you will find understanding, which makes us sharers in the wisdom of God's Son by understanding and knowing his will, a will that wants nothing but that we be made holy. When we see this, our soul cannot be sad or shaken, no matter what happens, for we know that everything is done with God's providence and tremendous love.

I want you, I beg you for love of the slain Lamb, to use this knowledge to assuage the grief and heartache you have felt because of Stefano's departure. Be glad; be happy! For this will surely make his soul and yours grow in grace. And by God's grace you will see him soon.

Getting back to self-knowledge: I tell you, you will also find there the gentle mercy of the Holy Spirit, the aspect of God that gives and is nothing but love. Whatever the Spirit does is done because of love. And this movement of love you will find within your own soul, because our will is nothing but love, and its every affection and movement comes from nothing but love. It loves or hates whatever the eye of understanding has seen and understood. How true it is then, dearest mother, that within the cell of your soul you will find the whole of God. And he bestows such sweetness, refreshment, and consolation that no matter what may happen we cannot be shaken, because we have been made big enough to hold God's own will. How? By getting rid of all selfish love, by getting rid of everything that is not God's will.

Then right away our soul is transformed into a garden filled with fragrant blossoms of holy desire.

And in the center of the garden is planted the tree of the most holy cross, the resting place of the spotless Lamb. He bathes and waters this glorious garden, irrigating it with his blood; and he himself bears the mature fruit of true solid virtues. If you want patience, he is the bedrock of meekness, since not a murmur of complaint was heard from the Lamb. He is the bedrock of deep humility, since God stooped down to humanity, and the Word stooped to the shameful death of the cross. If you want charity, he is that charity—and even more, for it was the power of love and charity that kept him nailed fast to the cross. The cross and nails could never have held the God-Man, had not the power of charity held him. I'm not surprised that those who make of themselves a garden through self-knowledge are strong in the face of the whole world, for they are conformed and made one with supreme strength. They truly begin in this life to have a foretaste of eternal life. They control the world by making light of it. The devils are afraid to get near a soul on fire with divine charity.

So up, dearest mother! I don't want you sleeping any more in irresponsibility and sensual love. No, with a boundless blazing love get up and take a bath in Christ's blood, hide in the wounds of Christ crucified. I'll say no more. I'm sure that if you live in the cell I've been talking about you will discover none other than Christ crucified. And tell Corrado to do the same. Keep living in God's holy and tender love.

Gentle Jesus! Jesus love!

PRAYER

From a letter (T353) to Monna Catella and others in
Naples (spring 1379)

*Little is known of the group of women to whom this letter
was addressed. Catherine wrote a similar letter to a niece
about the same time, so perhaps it is general advice she felt
moved to send to various disciples. In this section, she talks
about various kinds of prayer.*

There are three ways of praying. The first is that
abiding holy desire which prays to God in everything
we creatures do, for it directs all our spiritual and
bodily actions in his honor, and so is called continu-
ous. The glorious Saint Paul seems to have meant this
kind of prayer when he said: "Pray without ceasing."
Then there is vocal prayer, as when the tongue is used
in reciting the Office or other vocal prayers. This is a
preparation for the third kind of prayer, namely mental, which the soul comes to when it practices vocal
prayer prudently and humbly; that is when, as the
tongue prays, the heart is not far from God.

But one must endeavor to establish the heart
firmly in a love for divine Charity. And whenever one
feels God visiting one's mind, drawing it in some way
to think of the Creator, one should stop praying
vocally and rest lovingly in whatever one feels this
visitation to be. If there is still time when this has

passed, the soul should resume its vocal prayer so that the mind will always be full and not empty. And even if the prayer abounds in battles of all kinds, in darkness and great confusion of mind, with the devil suggesting that our prayer is not pleasing to God, we must not give up prayer on this account, but persist with fortitude and unfailing perseverance, realizing that this is the devil's way of enticing us away from our mother, prayer; and that God permits this to test in us our fortitude and constancy and also so that, in the struggles and darkness, we may know our own nothingness, while in the good will that we perceive in ourselves we know the goodness of God, who gives and upholds our good and holy desires, and will not refuse this gift to those who ask him.

The soul thus comes to the third and last kind of fully mental prayer, in which it receives the fruit of the efforts it has put into the less perfect vocal prayer, for it now savors the milk of fidelity to prayer. It lifts itself above the crude level of feeling and with the mind as of an angel is made one with God by love; by the light of its understanding it sees, knows and is clothed with the Truth. Made now sister to the angels, seated with the Bridegroom at the table of crucified desire, it delights in seeking God's honor and the salvation of souls for which, it now sees clearly, the eternal Bridegroom ran to meet the shameful death of the cross and, in so doing, obeyed his Father's will and achieved our salvation. Such prayer is indeed a mother, conceiving her children, the virtues, in God's love, and giving birth to them in love for others. Where do you find the light that guides you in the way of truth? In prayer. And where do you display love, faith, hope and humility? Again, in prayer. You would not be doing these things unless you loved them, and it is because a creature loves that it seeks to be one with the thing it loves, that is, with God. By prayer you ask him for what you need. Knowing yourself—and true prayer is founded on this knowledge—you see you are in great need and feel surrounded by your enemies: the world with its hurts; the devil, with all his temptations; and the flesh, ever warring against the spirit by rebelling against reason. You see, too, that of yourself you are not; and since you are not, you cannot help yourself; so you turn with faith, to him who IS; who knows your needs and can and will help you in them. You ask with hope, then wait for his help. This is how we must pray if we are to get what we desire. No right thing will ever be denied us if we ask the divine Goodness for it in this way, but we would get very little benefit from praying in any other.

Where shall we sense the fragrance of obedience, if not in prayer? Where strip ourselves of the self-love that makes us impatient when insulted or made to suffer? Or put on a divine love that will make us patient, and ready to glory in the cross of Christ crucified? In prayer. And where shall we sense the sweet perfume of virginity and purity, and a

hunger for martyrdom that will make us ready to give
our lives for the honor of God and the salvation of
souls? In this sweet mother, prayer. She will make us
obey God's holy commandments, and seal her coun-
sels into our hearts and minds by imprinting on us the
desire to keep them until death. She withdraws us
from the company of creatures and gives us the
Creator as companion. She fills the vessel of our heart
with the blood of the humble spotless Lamb and
clothes it in Fire, for by the fire of Love was it shed.

LOVE AND
SERVICE

From *Dialogue*, Chapter 7

The Dialogue *is Catherine's only book, a summary of all her teaching, presented as a dialogue between an ardent soul and God. At least the core of the book was dictated while Catherine was caught up in ecstatic prayer. The soul begins with a series of questions and occasionally offers a prayer of thanksgiving, but in most of the book, including all but the last of these selections, God is the speaker. Here God speaks about service to neighbors. Note that Catherine always refers to the soul as "she."*

The soul sees that she can become grateful and acceptable to me in no other way than by conceiving hatred of sin and love of virtue. When she has thus conceived by the affection of love, she immediately gives birth to fruit for her neighbors. There is no other way that can she act out the truth she has conceived in herself except by loving me in truth. And in the same truth, she serves her neighbors.

And it cannot be otherwise because love of me and love of her neighbors are one and the same thing. So far as the soul loves me, she loves her neighbors because love toward them issues from me. This is the means that I have given you, so that you may exercise and prove your virtue. Since you can do me no service, you should do it to your neighbors. This proves that you possess me by grace in your soul: bearing much fruit for your neighbors and making prayers to me, seeking with sweet and loving desire my honor and the salvation of souls. The soul that is enamored of my truth never ceases to serve the whole world, both in general and in particular cases, according to the situation of the recipient and the ardent desire of the donor. As I showed you earlier, the endurance of suffering alone, without desire, was not enough to atone for sin.

When she has discovered the advantage of this unitive love in me, by means of which she truly loves herself, she extends her desire to the salvation of the whole world and seeks to come to the aid of its neediness. Just as she has done good to herself by the conception of virtue, from which she has drawn the life of grace, now she strives to fix her eye on the needs of her neighbor in particular. So when, through the affection of love, she has discovered the state of all rational creatures in general, she helps those who are at hand, according to the various graces that I have entrusted to her to administer. One she helps with doctrine, that is, with words, giving sincere counsel without any respect of persons. She helps another with the example of a good life. Indeed all can give their neighbors this much: the edification of a holy and honorable life. These virtues and many others — too many to list — are brought forth in the love of the neighbor. I have given them in different ways, that is to say not all to one, but to one, one virtue, and to another, another. But really it is impossible to have one, without having them all, because all the virtues are bound together. Understand, then, that in many cases I give one virtue, to be like the chief of the others. That is to say, to one I will give principally love, to another justice, to another humility, to one a lively faith, to another prudence or temperance or patience, to another fortitude. I place these and many other virtues in the souls of many creatures. So it happens that the particular one so placed in the soul becomes the principal object of its virtue. The soul disposes herself to this rather than to other virtues for her primary rule of conduct. By the effect of this virtue, the soul draws to herself all the other virtues, since they are all bound together in the affection of love. So it is with many gifts and graces of virtue — not only in the case of spiritual things but also of temporal. I use the word *temporal* for the things necessary to the physical life. All these I have given so that no one soul should have them all. Therefore you must show love, at least in material things, for one another. I could easily have created people possessed of all that they should need for both body and soul. But I wish one to have need of the other so that they should all be my ministers to administer the graces and the gifts that they have received from me. Whether they will or not, they cannot help making an act of love. It is true, however, that unless that act is made through love of me, it does them no good so far as grace is concerned.

See, then, that I have made people my ministers and placed them in various stations and ranks so that they may make use of the virtue of love. In my house are many mansions. I wish for nothing other than love, for love of me is fulfilled and completed in the love of the neighbors, and in this love the law is observed. For only those who are bound to me with this love can be of use, whatever their state of life.

The Bridge

From *Dialogue*, Chapter 26

The central image in the Dialogue *is of Christ as a Bridge connecting earth and heaven, crossing the river that human sin has caused to divide the two. People reach the Bridge by three steps that Catherine compares at various times to Christ's feet, wounded side, and mouth; to human memory, intellect, and will; and to stages of spiritual growth, which Catherine calls the imperfect, the perfect, and the more perfect.*

I will now explain to you the nature of this Bridge. I have told you, my daughter, that the Bridge reaches from heaven to earth. It does this through the union I have made with humanity, whom I formed of the clay of the earth. Now learn that this Bridge, my only begotten Son, has three steps. Two were made with the wood of the most holy cross, and the third still retains the great bitterness he tasted when he was given gall and vinegar to drink. In these three steps you will recognize three states of the soul, which I will explain to you below. The feet of the soul, signifying her affection, are the first step, for the feet carry the body as the affection carries the soul. So my Son's pierced feet are steps by which you can arrive at his side. His side shows you the secret of his heart because the soul, rising on the steps of her affection, commences to taste the love of his heart by gazing into that open heart of my Son with the eye of the intellect and finds it consumed with unspeakable love. I say consumed because he does not love you for his own benefit. You can be of no benefit to him, since he is one and the same thing with me. Then the soul is filled with love, seeing herself so much loved. Having passed the second step, the soul reaches out to the third. This is to the mouth, where she finds peace from the terrible war she has been waging with her sin. On the first step, then, lifting her feet from the affections of the earth, the soul strips herself of vice. On the second she fills herself with love and virtue. And on the third she tastes peace. So the Bridge has three steps, so that by climbing past the first and the second, you may reach the last. This is lifted high so that the water running beneath may not touch it. That is, there was no venom of sin touching my Son. This Bridge is lifted high and yet, at the same time, joined to the earth. Do you know when it was lifted high? When my Son was lifted up on the wood of the most holy cross. His divine nature remained joined to the lowliness of the earth of your humanity.

For this reason I said to you that even when he was lifted high, he was not lifted out of the earth. The divine nature is united and kneaded into one thing with it. And there was no one who could go on the Bridge until it had been lifted high. That is why he said, "If I am lifted high I will draw all things to me." When my goodness saw that in no other way could you be drawn to me, I sent him so that he should be lifted high on the wood of the cross. I made of it an anvil on which my Son, born of human generation, could be remade. I did this to free you from death and to restore you to the life of grace. And so he drew everything to himself by this means: by showing the unspeakable love with which I love you. For the human heart is always attracted by love. Greater love, then, I could not show you than to lay down my life for you. So my Son had to be treated in this way by love so that ignorant people should be unable to resist being drawn to me.

In very truth, then, my Son said that when he was lifted high, he would draw all things to himself. And this is to be understood in two ways. First, when the human heart is drawn by the affection of love, as I have said, it is drawn together with all the powers of his soul—with the memory, the intellect, and the will. Now, when these three powers are harmoniously joined together in my name, all the other operations that the soul performs—whether in deed or thought— are pleasing. They are joined together by the effect of love because love is lifted on high, following the sorrowful Crucified One. So my Truth said well, "If I am lifted high I will draw all things to me." If the heart and the powers of the soul are drawn to him, all the actions are also drawn to him. Second, everything has been created for the service of humanity, to serve the necessities of rational creatures. The rational creatures have not been made for them but for me, to serve me with all their hearts and with all their affection. See, then, that when you are drawn, everything else is drawn with you because everything else has been made for you. It was therefore necessary that the Bridge should be lifted on high and have steps, so that it might be climbed more easily.

RIVER AND THORNS

From *Dialogue*, Chapter 44

Here God speaks of how Satan tempts souls to avoid the Bridge—and so drown in the river. In another metaphor, these souls are scared away from the Tree of Life for fear of thorns that seem to surround it.

I have told you that the devil invites people to the water of death since that is what he himself has. Blinding them with the pleasures and conditions of the world, he catches them with the hook of pleasure under the pretense of good. There is no other way could he catch them, for they would not allow themselves to be caught if they saw that they would get no good or pleasure from it. The soul naturally always desires the good. But indeed the soul, blinded by self-love, does not know and discern what is truly good and profitable to the soul and to the body. So the devil, seeing them blinded by self-love, evilly places before them various kinds of delights, colored so as to have the appearance of some benefit or good. He gives to all according to their condition and those principal vices to which he sees them to be most disposed. He gives one kind to the laity, another to the religious, and others to priests and noblemen, according to their different conditions. I have told you this because I now speak to you of those who drown themselves in the river and care for nothing but themselves. They love themselves to my injury. Now I will tell you their end.

I want to show you how they deceive themselves and how, wishing to flee troubles, they fall into them. Because it seems to them that following me — that is, walking by the way of the Bridge, the Word, my Son — is great toil, they draw back. They fear the thorns because they are blinded and do not know or see the truth. You know that I showed you this in the beginning of your life, when you prayed for me to have mercy on the world and draw it out of the darkness of mortal sin. You know that I then showed you myself under the figure of a tree, of which you saw neither the bottom nor the top. You could not see that the roots were united with the earth of your humanity. At the foot of the tree, if you remember well, there was a certain thorn. All those who loved their own sensuality kept away from it. Instead, they ran to a mountain of chaff that you recognized as a figure for all the delights of the world. That chaff mountain seemed to be of wheat. But it was not, and so, as you saw, many souls died of hunger on it. Many others recognized the deceits of the world and returned to the tree and passed the thorns, which is the decision of the will. Before this decision is made, it is a thorn that appears to stand in the way of following the truth. Conscience always fights on one side and sensuality on the other. But as soon as they, with hatred and displeasure toward themselves, bravely make up

their minds, saying, "I wish to follow Christ crucified," they immediately break through the thorns and
find inestimable sweetness, as I showed you then.
Some find more and some less, according to their dis-
position and desire. And you know that then I said to
you, "I am your God, unmoving and unchangeable. I
do not draw away from any creature who wants to
come to me."

I have shown them the truth, making myself visi-
ble to them. I have shown them what it is to love anything apart from me. But they, as if blinded by the fog
of disordered love, know neither me nor themselves.
You see how deceived they are. They choose to die of
hunger rather than to pass a little thorn bush. But
they cannot escape enduring pain. No one can pass
through this life without a cross. How much less
those who travel by the lower way! Not that my servants pass without pain. But their pain is eased. And
because—by sin, as I said to you above—the world
brings forth thorns and tribulations, and because this
river flows with tempestuous waters, I gave you the
Bridge, so that you might not be drowned.

BEGINNING TO CLIMB

From *Dialogue*, Chapters 59–60

In this selection, God explains the three steps as stages in the spiritual life. They are described here as imperfect, perfect, and more perfect and seem to correspond with the more traditional stages of purgation, enlightenment, and union. Here the emphasis is on the pitfalls of the first two stages.

I told you that no one could go by the Bridge or come out of the river without climbing the three steps. This is the truth. There are some who climb imperfectly, and some perfectly, and some climb with the greatest perfection. The first are those who are moved by slavish fear. Though they have climbed this far, they are imperfectly gathered together. That is to say, the soul has seen the punishment that follows her sin. So she climbs and gathers together her memory to recollect her vice, her intellect to see the punishment she expects to receive for her fault, and her will to move her to hate that fault. Let us consider this to be the first step and the first gathering together of the powers of the soul. It should be taken by the light of the intellect. The mind's eye, whose pupil is holy faith, looks not only at the punishment of sin, but at the fruit of virtue and the love that I bear to the soul. So she may climb with love and affection, stripped of slavish fear. In doing so, such souls will become faithful and not unfaithful servants. They serve me through love and not through fear. If, with hatred of sin, they employ their minds to dig out the root of their self-love with prudence, constancy, and perseverance, they will succeed in doing so. But there are many who begin their course climbing so slowly and render their debt to me by such small degrees and with such negligence and ignorance that they suddenly faint. Every little breeze catches their sails and turns their prow backward. Since they imperfectly climb to the first step of the Bridge of Christ crucified, they do not arrive at the second step of his heart.

There are some who have become faithful servants, serving me with fidelity and love rather than slavish fear of punishment. But if they serve me with a view to their own profit or the delight and pleasure that they find in me, even this love is imperfect. Do you know what proves the imperfection of this love? The withdrawal of the consolations that they found in me, and the insufficiency and short duration of their love for their neighbor. It grows weak bit by bit and sometimes disappears. Their love toward me grows weak when, on occasion, in order to test them in virtue and raise them above their imperfection, I withdraw my consolation from their minds and allow them to fall into battles and confusion. I do this so that they may come to perfect self-knowledge and know that they are nothing and have no grace of themselves. Accordingly in time of battle they will fly to me, their benefactor, seeking me alone with true humility. That is why I treat them this way, withdrawing consolation from them indeed but not grace. At such a time these weak ones of whom I speak relax their energy and impatiently turn backward. Sometimes they abandon many of their exercises and call this virtue. They say to themselves, *This labor does me no good.* They do all this because they feel themselves deprived of mental consolation. Such a soul acts imperfectly, for she has not yet unwound the bandage of spiritual self-love. Had she unwound it she would see that, in truth, everything comes from me. No leaf of a tree falls to the ground without my providence, and what I give and promise to my creatures, I give and promise to them for their sanctification. This is the good and the end for which I created them. My creatures should see and know that I wish nothing but their good, through the blood of my only begotten Son, in which they are washed from their iniquities. By this blood they are enabled to know my truth: how, in order to give them eternal life, I created them in my image and likeness and re-created them by grace with the blood of my Son, making them my children by adoption. But since they are imperfect, they make use of me only for their own benefit, relaxing their love for their neighbor. So those in the first state come to nothing through the fear of enduring pain. Those in the second also come to nothing because they slacken their pace, cease to render service to their neighbor, and withdraw their charity if they see their own profit or consolation withdrawn from them. This happens because their love was originally impure. They gave to their neighbor the same imperfect love that they gave to me: a love based only on desire for their own advantage. If, through a desire for perfection, they do not recognize their imperfection, it is impossible that they should not turn back. For those who desire eternal life, a pure love without any selfish regard is necessary. It is not enough for eternal life to fly from sin out of fear of punishment or to embrace virtue from the motive of one's own advantage. Sin should be abandoned because it is displeasing to me, and virtue should be loved for my sake.

fROM VOCAL TO
MENTAL PRAYER

From *Dialogue*, Chapter 66

In this selection, God speaks of the need to go beyond saying written or memorized prayers (vocal prayer) to prayer that comes from one's own heart and mind (mental prayer). Only such prayer can truly stir and illuminate the soul.

Do not think that the soul receives such ardor and nourishment from prayer if she prays only vocally, as do many souls whose prayers are words rather than love. These only care about completing psalms and saying many Our Fathers. Once they have completed their appointed tally, they do not appear to think of anything further. They seem to place devout attention and love in merely vocal recitation. The soul is not required to do this. And in doing only this she bears but little fruit, and that pleases me very little. But if you ask me whether the soul should abandon vocal prayer (since it does not seem to all that they are called to mental prayer), I should reply, "No." The soul should advance step by step. I know well that, just as the soul is at first imperfect and afterward perfect, so it is with her prayer also. She should still continue in vocal prayer while she is imperfect, so as not to fall into idleness. But she should not say her vocal prayers without joining them to mental prayer. That is, while she is reciting she should endeavor to raise her mind in my love, considering her own sins and the blood of my only begotten Son, in which she finds the breadth of my charity and the remission of her sins. She should do this so that self-knowledge and the consideration of her defects will make her recognize my goodness in herself and continue her exercises with true humility. I do not wish sins to be considered in particular but in general so that the mind may not be contaminated by the remembrance of particular and hideous sins. But, as I said, I do not wish the soul to consider her sins, either in general or in particular, without also remembering the blood and the broadness of my mercy. Otherwise she might be brought to confusion. And together with confusion would come the devil, who has caused it, under guise of remorse and displeasure for sin. So she would arrive at eternal damnation, not only on account of her confusion, but also through the despair that would come to her because she did not seize the arm of my mercy.

The soul, therefore, should season the knowledge of herself with the knowledge of my goodness. Then vocal prayer will be of use to the soul who makes it, and pleasing to me. And she will arrive from the vocal imperfect prayer, exercised with perseverance, at perfect mental prayer. But if she simply aims at completing her tally and abandons mental prayer for vocal, she will never arrive at it. Sometimes I may visit the soul's mind, sometimes in one way, and sometimes in another, in a flash of self-knowledge or of contrition for sin, sometimes in the broadness of my charity. Sometimes I may place the presence of my truth before her mind, in various ways and according to my pleasure and the desire of the soul. But the soul will be so ignorant that, having resolved to say so many prayers vocally, she will abandon my visitation (that she feels by conscience), rather than abandon what she had begun. She should not do so, for, in so doing, she yields to a deception of the devil. The moment she feels her mind disposed by my visitation (in the many ways I have told you), she should abandon vocal prayer. Then when my visitation is past and if there is time, she can resume the vocal prayers that she had resolved to say. But if she has not time to complete them, she ought not on that account to be troubled or suffer annoyance and confusion of mind.

You see, then, that perfect prayer is reached not through many words, but through affection of desire. The soul raises herself to me with knowledge of herself and of my mercy, each one adding to the flavor of the other. Thus she will engage in both mental and vocal prayer. For just as the active and contemplative life are one, so are they. Of course, vocal or mental prayer can be understood in many different ways. I have told you that a holy desire is a continual prayer. A good and holy will disposes itself with desire to the occasion actually appointed for prayer in addition to the continual prayer of holy desire itself. So vocal prayer will be made at the appointed time by the soul who remains firm in a habitual holy will. Sometimes it will even be continued beyond the appointed time, as love commands for the salvation of others (if the soul sees them to be in need), and also her own necessities according to the state in which I have placed her. Each soul, according to her condition, ought to exert herself for the salvation of souls, for this exercise lies at the root of a holy will. Whatever she may contribute, by words or deeds, toward the salvation of her neighbors is virtually a prayer. This is what my glorious standard-bearer Paul said, in the words, "Whoever does not stop working does not stop praying." It was for this reason that I told you that prayer was made in many ways, that is, that actual prayer may be united with mental prayer if made with the affection of love. And this love is itself continual prayer.

 GOING ON TO
PERFECTION

From *Dialogue*, Chapters 99–100

Here the discussion moves to the third stage of spiritual growth, as the soul moves to ever greater perfection and union with God. This means moving from the light of reason that sees the transitory nature of the world to the light of faith that sees God's love and goodness. Here, too, there are pitfalls.

When the soul has attained this general light, of which I have spoken, she should not remain contented. As long as you are pilgrims in this life, you are capable of growth. Whoever does not go forward, by that very fact is turning back. The soul should either grow in the general light, which she has acquired through my grace, or anxiously strive to attain to the second and perfect light, leaving the imperfect and reaching the perfect. For if the soul truly has light, it will wish to arrive at perfection. In this second perfect light are to be found two kinds of perfection—for those who have abandoned the general way of living of the world may be called perfect. One perfection is that of those who give themselves completely to subduing bodily desires by doing great and severe penance. These, in order that their sensuality may not rebel against their reason, have placed their desire rather in the mortification of the body than in the destruction of their self-will, as I have explained to you in another place. They feed their souls at the table of penance and are good and perfect, if their penance is illuminated by discretion and founded on me— that is, if they act with true knowledge of themselves and of me, with great humility, and are wholly conformed to the judgment of my will, and not to the human will's judgment. But if they were not thus clothed with my will and in true humility, they would often offend against their own perfection, esteeming themselves the judges of those who do not walk in the same path. Do you know why this would happen to them? Because they have placed all their labor and desire in the mortification of the body rather than in the destruction of their own will.

Such as these wish always to choose their own times and places and consolations, after their own fashion, and also the persecutions of the world and of the devil. They cheat themselves with the delusion of their own "spiritual" self-will when they say, "I wish to have that consolation, and not these battles, or these temptations of the devil, not, indeed, for my own pleasure, but in order to please God more and in order to hold him more in my soul through grace. It seems to me that I should possess him more and serve him better in that way than in this." And this is the way the soul often falls into trouble and becomes tedious and unbearable to herself. In this way she injures her own perfection. She still does not perceive this injury or that the stench of pride lurks within her. And there she lies.

Now if the soul were not in this condition but were truly humble and not presumptuous, she would be illuminated to see that I, the First Sweet Truth, grant condition and time and place and consolations and tribulations as they may be needed for your salvation and to complete the perfection I have chosen for the soul. And she would see that I give everything through love. Therefore, she should receive everything with love and reverence. That is what the souls in the second state do. By doing this, they arrive at the third state. I will now speak to you about them, explaining to you the nature of these two states, which stand in the most perfect light.

The third state immediately follows the last, and those who belong to it and have arrived at this glorious light are perfect in every condition in which they may be. They receive every event that I permit to happen to them with due reverence, as I have mentioned to you when speaking of the third and unitive state of the soul. These deem themselves worthy of the troubles and stumbling blocks caused them by the world and of the privation of their own consolation and indeed of whatever circumstance happens to them. Since they deem themselves worthy of trouble, so also do they deem themselves unworthy of the fruit, which they receive after their trouble. In the light they have known and tasted my eternal will that wishes nothing else but your good and gives and permits these troubles so that you should be sanctified in me. So the soul that has known my will clothes herself with it and fixes her attention on nothing else except seeing in what way she can preserve and increase her perfection to the glory and praise of my name. She opens the eye of her intellect and fixes it in the light of faith upon Christ crucified, my only begotten Son. She loves and follows his teaching, which is the rule of the road for perfect and imperfect alike. And see how my Truth, the Lamb, who became enamored of her when he saw her, gives the soul the doctrine of perfection. She knows what this perfection is since she has seen it practiced by the sweet and amorous Word, my only begotten Son, who was fed at the table of holy desire, seeking honor and your salvation from me, the eternal Father. And inflamed with this desire, he ran with great eagerness to the shameful death of the Cross, and accomplished the obedience that was imposed on him by me, his Father. He did not shun labors or insults or withdraw on account of your ingratitude or ignorance of so great a benefit or because of the persecutions of the Jews or on account of the insults, derision, grumbling, and shouting of the people. But all this he passed through like the true captain and knight that he was. For I had placed him on the battlefield to deliver you from the hands of the devil so that you might be set free and drawn out of the most terrible slavery in which you could ever be and also to teach you his road, his doctrine, and his rule. In this way you might open the door of me, Eternal Life, with the key of his precious blood, shed with such fire of love and such hatred of your sins. It was as if the sweet and loving Word, my Son, had said to you: "Behold, I have made the road and opened the door with my blood." So do not be negligent to follow, laying yourselves down to rest in self-love and ignorance of the road, presuming to choose to serve me in your own way, instead of in the way that I have made straight for you by means of my Truth, the incarnate Word, and built up with his blood. Rise up then promptly, and follow him, for no one can reach me, the Father, if not by him; he is the Way and the Door by which you must enter into me, the Sea of Peace.

PERFECT PURITY

As the discussion of perfection continues, Catherine is reminded of an earlier vision in which Christ had pointed the way to purity through refusing to judge others.

Do you want to arrive at perfect purity and be freed from stumbling blocks so that your mind may not be scandalized by anything? Unite yourself always to me by the affection of love, for I am the Supreme and Eternal Purity. I am the Fire that purifies the soul. The closer the soul is to me, the purer she becomes. The farther she is from me, the more her purity leaves her. This is why people of the world fall into such iniquities, for they are separated from me. But the soul who, without any intermediary, unites herself directly to me participates in my purity.

Another thing is necessary for you to arrive at this union and purity: that you should never judge the human will in anything that you may see done or said by any creature whatsoever, either to yourself or to others. You should consider my will alone, both in them and in yourself. And if you should see evident sins or defects, draw the rose out of those thorns. That is to say, offer them to me with holy compassion. In the case of injuries done to yourself, judge that my

will permits this in order to prove virtue in yourself
and in my other servants, figuring that the one who
acts thus does so as the instrument of my will. You
should also realize that such apparent sinners may
frequently have a good intention. No one can judge
the secrets of a person's heart. What you do not see
you should not judge in your mind, even though it
may evidently be open mortal sin. See nothing in
others but my will—not in order to judge but, as has
been said, with holy compassion.

In this way you will arrive at perfect purity
because when you act this way, your mind will not be
scandalized either in me or in your neighbors. Otherwise you fall into contempt of your neighbors if you
judge their evil will toward you instead of my will act-
ing in them. Such contempt and scandal separate the
soul from me and prevent perfection and, in some
cases, deprive her of grace, more or less according to
the gravity of her contempt and the hatred her judgment has conceived against her neighbor.

A different reward is received by the soul who
perceives only my will. As has been said, it wishes
nothing else but your good so that everything I give
or permit to happen to you, I give so that you may
arrive at the end for which I created you. And because
the soul remains always in the love of her neighbor,
she remains always in my love and thus remains united to me. So in order to arrive at purity you must
entreat me to grant you three things: to be united to

me by the affection of love, retaining in your memory the benefits you have received from me; to see the affection of my love (with which I love you inestimably) with the eye of your intellect; and to discern my will only in the will of others and not their evil will. For I am their judge, not you, and in doing this you will arrive at all perfection.

fiNAL
pRAYER

From *Dialogue*, Chapter 167

The Dialogue *concludes with the soul's great outpouring of thanks for all that God has showed her and done for her.*

Thanks, thanks to you, O eternal Father, for you have not despised me, the work of your hands, or turned your face from me, or despised my desires. You, the Light, have not regarded my darkness. You, True Life, have not regarded my living death. You, the Physician, have not been repelled by my grave infirmities. You, the Eternal Purity, have not considered the many miseries of which I am full. You, who are the Infinite, have overlooked that I am finite. You, who are Wisdom, have overlooked my folly. Your wisdom, your goodness, your clemency, your infinite good, have overlooked these infinite evils and sins and the many others that are in me. Having known the truth through your clemency, I have found your charity and the love of my neighbors. What has constrained me? Not my virtues but only your charity. May that same charity constrain you to illuminate the eye of my intellect with the light of faith so that I may know and understand the truth that you have manifested to me. Grant that my memory may be capable of retaining your benefits and that my will may burn in the fire of your charity. May that fire so work in me that I give my body to be wounded, and that by my blood given for love of the blood of Christ, the key of obedience, I may unlock the door of heaven. I ask this of you with all my heart, for every rational creature, both in general and in particular, in the mystical body of the holy church. I confess and do not deny that you loved me before I existed. Your love for me is unspeakable, as if you were mad with love for your creature. Oh, eternal Trinity! O Godhead that gave value to the blood of your Son! You, O eternal Trinity, are a deep Sea. The deeper I enter the more I find, and the more I find the more I seek. The soul cannot be filled in your abyss, for she continually hungers after you, the eternal Trinity, desiring to see you with light in your light. As the deer desires the spring of living water, so my soul desires to leave the prison of this dark body and see you in truth.

How long, O eternal Trinity, fire and abyss of love, will your face be hidden from my eyes? Melt at once the cloud of my body. The knowledge that you have given me of yourself in your truth constrains me to long to abandon the heaviness of my body and to give my life for the glory and praise of your name. I have tasted and seen with the light of the intellect in your light, the abyss of you, the eternal Trinity, and the beauty of your creature. Looking at myself in you, I saw myself to be your image. My life was given me by your power, O eternal Father. Your wisdom, which

belongs to your only begotten Son, shines in my intellect and my will, being one with your Holy Spirit,
who proceeds from you and your Son and by whom I
am able to love you. You, eternal Trinity, are my
Creator, and I am the work of your hands. And I
know through the new creation you have given me in
the blood of your Son that you are enamored of the
beauty of your workmanship.

O Abyss, O eternal Godhead, O deep Sea!
What more could you give me than yourself? You are
the fire that ever burns without being consumed. You
consume in your heat all the soul's self-love. You are
the fire that takes away all cold.

With your light you illuminate me so that I may
know all your truth. You are the light above all light
that supernaturally illuminates the eye of my intellect,
clarifying the light of faith so abundantly and so perfectly that I see that my soul is alive and in this light
receives you, the true Light. By the light of faith I
have acquired wisdom in the wisdom of the Word,
your only begotten Son. In the light of faith I am
strong, constant, and persevering. In the light of faith
I hope. Do not allow me to faint by the way. This light,
without which I should still walk in darkness, teaches
me the road. For this I said, O eternal Father, that
you have illuminated me with the light of holy faith.

Truly this light is a sea, for the soul revels in
you, eternal Trinity, the Sea of Peace. The water of
the sea is not murky and causes no fear to the soul,

for she knows the truth. It is a deep that manifests sweet secrets so that where the light of your faith abounds, the soul is certain of what she believes. This water is a magic mirror into which you, the eternal Trinity, bid me gaze. You hold it with the hand of love so that I may see myself, your creature, there represented in you and yourself in me through the union that you made of your Godhead with our humanity. For this light I know to represent to myself you—the supreme and infinite Good, Good blessed and incomprehensible, Good inestimable. Beauty above all beauty; Wisdom above all wisdom—for you are Wisdom itself. You, the food of the angels, have given yourself in a fire of love to people. You, the garment that covers all our nakedness, feed the hungry with your sweetness. Oh! Sweet, without any bitter, O eternal Trinity!

In your light you have given me with the light of holy faith I have known the many and wonderful things you have declared to me. You explained to me the path of supreme perfection so that I may no longer serve you in darkness, but with light, and that I may be the mirror of a good and holy life, and arise from my miserable sins, for through them I have hitherto served you in darkness. I have not known your truth and have not loved it. Why did I not know you? Because I did not see you with the glorious light of the holy faith; because the cloud of self-love darkened the eye of my intellect. But you, the eternal

Trinity, have dissipated the darkness with your light. Who can attain to your greatness? Who can give you thanks for such immeasurable gifts and benefits as you have given me in this doctrine of truth? It has been a special grace over and above the ordinary graces that you give also to your other creatures. You have been willing to condescend to my need and to that of your creatures—the need of introspection. Having first given the grace to ask the question, you reply to it and satisfy your servant, penetrating me with a ray of grace so that in that light I may give you thanks. Clothe me, clothe me with you, O eternal Truth, so that I may run my mortal course with true obedience and the light of holy faith. I feel that my soul is about to become drunk again with that light. Amen.

appendix

Reading Spiritual Classics for Personal and Group Formation

Many Christians today are searching for more spiritual depth, for something more than simply being good church members. That quest may send them to the spiritual practices of New Age movements or of Eastern religions such as Zen Buddhism. Christians, though, have their own long spiritual tradition, a tradition rich with wisdom, variety, and depth.

The great spiritual classics testify to that depth. They do not concern themselves with mystical flights for a spiritual elite. Rather, they contain very practical advice and insights that can support and shape the spiritual growth of any Christian. We can all benefit by sitting at the feet of the masters (both male and female) of Christian spirituality.

Reading spiritual classics is different from most of the reading we do. We have learned to read to master a text and extract information from it. We tend to read quickly, to get through a text. And we summarize as we read, seeking the main point. In reading spiritual classics, though, we allow the text to master and form us. Such formative reading goes more slowly, more reflectively, allowing time for God to speak to us through the text. God's word for us may come as easily from a minor point or even an aside as from the major point.

Formative reading requires that you approach the text in humility. Read as a seeker, not an expert. Don't demand that the text meet your expectations for what an "enlightened" author should write. Humility means accepting the author as another imperfect human, a product of his or her own time and situation. Learn to celebrate what is foundational in an author's writing without being overly disturbed by what is peculiar to the author's life and times. Trust the text as a gift from both God and the author, offered to you for your benefit—to help you grow in Christ.

To read formatively, you must also slow down. Feel free to reread a passage that seems to speak specially to you. Stop from time to time to reflect on what you have been reading. Keep a journal for these reflections. Often the act of writing can itself prompt further, deeper reflection. Keep your notebook open and your pencil in hand as you read. You might not get back to that wonderful insight later. Don't worry that you are not getting through an entire passage— or even the first paragraph! Formative reading is about depth rather than breadth, quality rather than quantity. As you read, seek God's direction for your own life. Timeless truths have their place but may not be what is most important for your own formation here and now.

As you read the passage, you might keep some of these questions running through your mind:

• How is what I'm reading true of my own life? Where does it reflect my own *experience*?

• How does this text challenge me? What new *direction* does it offer me?

• What must I change to put what I am reading into practice? How can I *incarnate* it, let this word become flesh in my life?

You might also devote special attention to sections that upset you. What is the source of the disturbance? Do you want to argue theology? Are you turned off by cultural differences? Or have you been skewered by an insight that would turn your life upside down if you took it seriously? Let your journal be a dialogue with the text.

If you find yourself moving from reading the text to chewing over its implications to praying, that's great! Spiritual reading is really the first step in an ancient way of prayer called *lectio divina* or "divine reading." Reading leads naturally into reflection on what you have read (meditation). As you reflect on what the text might mean for your life, you may well want to ask for God's help in living out any new insights or direction you have perceived (prayer). Sometimes such prayer may lead you further into silently abiding in God's presence (contemplation). And, of course, the process is only really completed when it begins to make a difference in the way we live (incarnation).

As good as it is to read spiritual classics in solitude, it is even better to join with others in a small group for mutual formation or "spiritual direction in